WILDLIFE IN BLOOM SERIES

Little Rabbit

BY AUTHOR & CONSERVATIONIST

LINDA BLACKMOOR

ISBN: 978-1-966417-18-7 (PRINT)

PUBLISHED BY QUILL PRESS. LINDA BLACKMOOR'S TITLES MAY BE PURCHASED IN BULK FOR EDUCATIONAL, BUSINESS, FUNDRAISING, OR SALES PROMOTIONAL USE. FOR INFORMATION, PLEASE EMAIL HELLO@LINDABLACKMOOR.COM

FIRST PRINT EDITION: 2025

LINDA BLACKMOOR
WWW.LINDABLACKMOOR.COM

SPECIES

Rabbits are small mammals in the Leporidae family, which also includes hares. There are more than 300 kinds of rabbits, from wild cottontails to different pet breeds. They live on every continent except Antarctica and can handle many environments, like forests, grasslands, and deserts. Their variety in color, size, and fur shows how well they can adapt.

VISION

Rabbits have wide-set eyes giving them almost 360-degree vision to watch for danger. They see best in dim light like dawn and dusk, which is when they're most active. They have a tiny blind spot right in front of their nose. This special eyesight helps rabbits detect enemies, like foxes or hawks, from nearly every angle.

DIET

As herbivores, rabbits eat grasses, leaves, and veggies, using a special stomach part called the cecum to break down tough plants. They also do something called coprophagy, which means they eat certain droppings to get more nutrients. Their tummies must keep moving, so they need lots of hay or grass to stay healthy. This clever system helps them get every bit of energy from their food.

TEETH

Rabbit teeth never stop growing, adding about 3–5 inches (7–12 cm) a year if not worn down. Chewing on grass, hay, or safe wooden toys keeps them at the right length. Overgrown teeth can hurt a rabbit's mouth, making it hard to eat. Constant chewing is a key part of their healthy, plant-eating life.

BEHAVIOUR

Rabbits are often crepuscular, meaning they're busiest at dawn and dusk. A happy rabbit might do a joyful leap called a binky, twisting in midair to show excitement. When scared, they might stay perfectly still, hoping their natural colors hide them. These behaviors help them find food, interact with friends, and avoid hungry predators.

RABBIT FACTS #6

HABITAT

Wild rabbits live in many habitats, such as meadows, forests, and even deserts, looking for thick plants to hide in. They dig burrows called warrens underground, which protect them from bad weather and animals that want to eat them. These tunnels can have several rooms for sleeping or nesting. By changing their surroundings, rabbits stay safe and comfortable.

BABIES

Rabbits are fast breeders, with mothers (does) having multiple litters of babies (kits) each year. They carry their babies for about 28–31 days before giving birth. Newborn kits are blind and have no fur, but they grow quickly and start eating solid food in a few weeks. Having lots of babies helps rabbits survive even when predators are around.

RABBIT FACTS #8

SOCIAL

Some rabbits live in groups called colonies, with a boss rabbit leading and others following. They groom each other, share watching duties, and dig communal burrows to stay safe. This friendly living style lowers the risk of fights and helps them find more food. Working together makes life easier for the whole rabbit family.

PREDATOR

Many animals, like foxes, hawks, and snakes, love to hunt rabbits for food. Rabbits stay safe by running fast, hopping in zigzag patterns, and freezing in place to blend into the background. Their big ears warn them of danger, and strong back legs give them powerful jumps. Fast breeding is another way they keep their numbers up.

VOCALS

Rabbits use body language and quiet sounds to communicate with each other. They may thump a back foot on the ground to signal danger, or quietly grind their teeth when happy. Rabbits can also mark spots with scents from their chin or urine to say "this place is mine." These clues help them share news and protect their turf.

JUMP

Rabbits have mighty hind legs that let them jump up to 3 feet (1 meter) high and 10 feet (3 meters) forward. Their long feet and strong muscles help them leap away from threats and hop over obstacles. Some rabbits can even jump competitively, showing off how far and fast they can go. This skill is key to staying safe in wide-open spaces.

DOMESTIC

Rabbits were first raised for their meat and fur, and later became beloved pets kept for companionship. Monks in medieval Europe began careful breeding to create different colors and sizes, starting a long history of domestic breeds. Now, over 50 breeds exist, each with unique looks, like fluffy Angoras or tiny Netherland Dwarfs. Around the world, people adore rabbits for their gentle and playful nature.

EARS

A rabbit's ears can be very long, sometimes over 4 inches (10 cm), and help them hear threats and cool off. They can twist these ears in different directions to find out exactly where a sound is coming from. Blood flows through the ears to release heat when it's hot. Lop-eared rabbits have ears that hang down, which is just one of the many ways rabbits can look.